Jacob Have I Loved

Pamela Haught Stuart

authorHOUSE™

1663 LIBERTY DRIVE, SUITE 200
BLOOMINGTON, INDIANA 47403
(800) 839-8640
WWW.AUTHORHOUSE.COM

First published by AuthorHouse 3/15/2006

ISBN: 1-4259-0074-7 (sc)

Printed in the United States of America
Bloomington, Indiana

This book is printed on acid-free paper.

Dedication

I would like to dedicate this book to Pastor David Copeland and his lovely wife, Pam. Thank you for loving my family when we were forsaken and praying without ceasing for us.

My prayer for my readers is 2 Thessalonians 1:11-12 "Wherefore also we pray always for you, that our God would count you worthy of this calling, and fulfill all the good pleasure of his goodness, and the work of faith with power: That the name of our Lord Jesus Christ may be glorified in you, and ye in him, according to the grace of our God and the Lord Jesus Christ."

Psalm 96:3 (New Living Translation) "Publish his glorious deeds among the nations. Tell everyone about the amazing things he does."

Introduction

One of the greatest joys in life is knowing that we are loved, loved for ourselves, and yes, loved in spite of ourselves. The love of God is the most precious gift to each of us. It is freely given and has no boundaries. God has loved us with an *everlasting* love. What a blessed comfort to know that as we busy ourselves with our daily routines that God's love is always with us. He also gives us a loving heart. As you read this daily devotional, may your spirit be refreshed in knowing that God loves you just as He loved Jacob. "For God so loved the world...." James Beach M.Ed.

Trials

1Peter 4:12-13 (NIV) "Dear friends, do not be surprised at the painful trial you are suffering, as though something strange were happening to you. But rejoice that you participate in the sufferings of Christ, so that you may be overjoyed when his glory is revealed."

Various trials test our faith and produce patience. As Christians we are called not only to believe in Him but also to suffer with Him. Therefore, it is good to embrace these trials, looking forward to the day when we shall become perfect in His sight.

On that day, we shall lack nothing and will be able to ask without reproach for wisdom which will carry us to godly choices. These outcomes will be perfected in Him and by Him for our well-being and ultimate peace. We also know that in Him dwells our perfection, while without Him exists nothing that will last for eternal purposes.

Additional Scriptures: Hebrews 2:10 James 1:2-5
    Matthew 11:28-30

Joy

Phil. 4:4 (KJV) "Rejoice in the Lord always and again I say rejoice."

1Peter 1:8 "Whom having not seen, ye love; in whom, though now ye see him not, yet believing, ye rejoice with joy unspeakable and full of glory,"

Lord, this middle-aged housewife is happy today because she is getting new appliances- a washer that remembers to spin and a dryer that promises not to burn the delicates. Happy? Yes, I'm happy and excited too! But I can't help but wonder how long my happiness over the new appliances will last? Hopefully, until I'm caught up on my laundry.

It gives me peace to know that the joy I carry in my heart because of You will carry me to the end of my life, not just to the end of the laundry. I am aware of this because it has carried me this far, through broken friendships, extreme grief, dysfunctional churches, and even the sadness that comes from time to time for no good reason.

I thank you, Lord, that possessing joy does not depend on life's circumstances but rather on the joy that comes from confidence in You. Because of Your ultimate sacrifice, I am assured that life on this earth will carry me to heavenly joy where my relationship with You will be consummated.

Additional Scriptures: John 3:29, John 15:11, Psalm 4:7, Psalm 16:11

Self-Acceptance

Psalm: 139:14 (a) (NIV) "I praise you because I am fearfully and wonderfully made; your works are wonderful, I know that full well."

For some women, shopping for clothes is recreation, even an enjoyable experience. However, for me it is more a journey into frustration. I have so much to consider: how do I cover those large familial hips, the tummy that popped out with menopausal weight gain, not to mention those burn scars that stubbornly promise never ever to leave or forsake me?

During these shopping excursions, I remind myself that perfection on this side of heaven is not possible. His word instructs me that I should be content in whatsoever state I find myself . I'm still working on this one; however, I know from experience that standing on His word always brings peace.

Additional Scriptures: 1Timothy: 6:6-8 Philippians: 4:11

Empty Nest

Hebrews 13:14 (KJV) "For here we have no continuing city, but we seek one to come."

When my four children left home, I managed to catch one of the worst cases of empty nest syndrome going around. I was left breathless with the suddenness of it all.

Our last "child" moved out a few years ago. I still find myself looking back on the child-rearing years and thinking, "Did that really happen?" It was so fast! Why didn't I spend more time with my children, play more, discipline less, and nurture more? Lord, could I go back just this once and fix my mistakes? Perhaps, I could make those formative years less stressful and more ideal for my children.

However, there are many things I have learned from my mistakes. Most important is that his grace is sufficient for my children. They are all doing just what they were raised to do, and that is to be independent adults. I am proud of all of them and their self-sufficiency. I also realize that in spite of me, rather than because of me, they have become wonderful people. The psalmist says it so much better than I ever could. (Psalm 39:7-8 (a) "And now, Lord, what do I wait for? My hope is in You. Deliver me from all my transgressions". Yes Lord, my hope indeed is in You and Your promise to deliver me from all my transgressions. And now it is time to let go of the past, resting on His bosom of forgiveness and hope for better tomorrows.

Additional Scriptures: Psalm 16:9, Job 6:8

Salvation

John 3:16 (KJV) "For God so loved the world that He gave His only begotten Son, that whoever believes in Him should not perish but have eternal life."

> Driven by love
> God came to man
> Salvation was in his hands.
> Agape love He gave of freely
> For those who will,
> Shall live eternally.

Salvation is the greatest gift ever given. All that is required for us to receive this gift is to believe on Him who died for our sins. Why do so many fight against it? Make yourself a promise today to pray for that unsaved friend, relative, or co-worker.

Additional Scriptures: John 3:16-21, Isaiah 61:10, Hebrews 5:9

Moving Mountains

Luke 11:2 (KJV) "Our *Father* which art in heaven, Hallowed be thy name. Thy kingdom come, Thy will be done, as in heaven, so in earth."

The Bible clearly states that God is our *Father* who dwells in heaven. Since He is our father, were we not then begat by Him? Theoretically speaking, we possess the genes the very DNA of God. Therefore, through Him and by Him we can perform anything, including moving mountains. Isn't God amazing?

Additional Scriptures: Matthew 17:20, 1John 3:9,
    Galatians 2:20

Fear

Psalm: 27:1 (NIV) "The LORD is my light and my salvation—whom shall I fear? The LORD is the stronghold of my life—of whom shall I be afraid?"

Lord, all too often I am fearful. I worry about the future for my children, the health of my parents, and, of course there's always the fear of car wrecks, big dogs, someone breaking into the house, and the fears go on and on. The Bible assures me that these fears can be replaced by having faith in you.

Yes, Lord may these fears which penetrate my heart trickle, seep, and flow out of my life. I cast them upon you. Now, I shall soar like an eagle, renewed and confident in You.

Additional Scriptures: Psalm 27:1-3, Numbers 6:26

Attributes of God

Exodus 3:14 (KJV) "And God said unto Moses, I AM THAT I AM: and he said, Thus shalt thou say unto the children of Israel, I AM hath sent me unto you."

I am understanding; I am strength; I am compassion. I provide; I forgive; I encourage and reward. I love with a never ending love. I am the Rose of Sharon and the Lily of the Valley. I am the Bright and Morning Star. I am the King of all kings. Who Am I?

I AM THAT I AM.

Additional Scriptures: Exodus 3:14-15, Song of Solomon 2:1

Love

1John 3:1-2 (NIV) "How great is the love the Father has lavished on us, that we should be called children of God!" And that is what we are! The reason the world does not know us is that it did not know him. Dear friends, now we are children of God, and what we will be has not yet been made known. But we know that when he appears, we shall be like him, for we shall see him as he is."

> Before I met God, I thought I knew love, but before I
> knew God, there was no love.
> I never knew love like this before I met my Savior. "For
> God is love and love is of God."

> I love that He forgives all my mistakes and teaches me
> to forgive others for the mistakes they make. For
> without forgiveness there is no love.

> I love the quiet time spent in prayer when I feel Jesus
> standing near, and I love that for love He gave His
> son who loved us all.

Most of all, I love the way He paid the highest ransom ever paid, and I love His resurrection on the third day.

Additional Scriptures: 1John 3:1-2, Matthew 28:1-10

Choices

Romans 8:38-40 (NIV) "For I am convinced that neither death nor life, neither angels nor demons, neither the present nor the future, nor any powers, neither height nor depth, nor anything else in all creation, will be able to separate us from the love of God that is in Christ Jesus our Lord."

Matthew 13:46 "Again, the kingdom of heaven is like a merchant seeking beautiful pearls, who, when he had found one pearl of great price, went and sold all that he had and bought it."

> Those who choose Christ have chosen
> the abundant life but not a life without
> heartache, grief, and strife. Yet those who
> choose Christ shall find that they have chosen
> the pearl of great price, eternal life. Won't you
> choose Him today?

Additional Scriptures: Romans 5:17, Psalm 133:3, Luke 7:48, Romans 8:38-39

Prayer for Comfort

Isaiah 51:12 (a) (KJV) "I, even I, am He who comforts you."

Lord, may the wind of your gentle Spirit come softly now and embrace me as a blanket around, with tenderness, compassion, and care. Comfort me, Lord, with Your rod and staff; comfort me as a mother comforts her child in sorrow. May the wind of your gentle spirit come softly now and wrap me in the comfort that comes only from you. May the wind of your gentle spirit come softly now.

Additional Scriptures: Isaiah 42:1 (a) (NKJV), James 4:10, Psalm 23:4

Blessings

Joshua 1:9 (NIV) "Have I not commanded you? Be strong and courageous. Do not be terrified; do not be discouraged, for the LORD your God will be with you wherever you go."

"Count your blessings name them one by one. Count your blessings it will surprise you what the Lord has done."
"Count Your Blessings" was a song I learned as a child during the early 50's in a comfy little Presbyterian church with magnificent stained glass windows. Little did I realize how much this inspiring song would mean to me in the not so distant future.

At the age of 15, I was in a serious car wreck. The car I was riding in became airborne and flew over an embankment landing forty-nine feet down, bottom up in a dry creek bed. I was trapped under the car while gasoline leaked onto my body. The car blew, and I was severely burned, suffering third degree burns over twenty-five percent of my body. I also had a crushed lung, a large laceration on my arm, and broken ribs. The pain was agonizing. To make matters worse, my burn specialist had a unique philosophy on pain medication. Simply put, he didn't believe in it. Every day for the first couple of weeks in the hospital, I endured debriefing. Debriefing involves taking something akin to a steel wool pad and vigorously scrubbing the burned area. Once the debriefing was finished, I was wrapped in clean gauze and soaked in silver nitrate. Silver nitrate is an acid, and while it was healing to the burns, the pain was excruciating. I learned after my first debriefing session that screaming didn't take me far. So I began singing, "Count your blessings, name them one by one, and it will *surprise* you what the Lord has done." I was *surprised*. I realized that while singing this song, God gave me both the courage and the strength to endure the trauma caused by the intense pain. I am reminded of soldiers who sing while going off to battle. It gives them courage. God indeed was mindful of me.

Additional Scriptures: Psalm 115:11-16,

No Wonder They Call Him God

Revelation 19:6 (KJV) "And I heard, as it were, the voice of a great multitude, as the sound of many waters and as the sound of mighty thunderings, saying, 'Alleluia! For the Lord God Omnipotent reigns!'"

A bush burns with holy fire, laws for living miraculously etched in stone. A donkey speaks; no wonder they call Him God.

Fire rains from the sky; frogs who moments before didn't exist multiply. Joshua marches seven times around; the walls of Jericho fall down; water turns to wine; a leper is healed.

A sea both deep and wide, suddenly divides; could this be why He is called Yahweh, God of nations; Lord of life, Jesus the Christ?

Additional Scriptures: Exodus 14:21-30, Deuteronomy 5:22-24

No Room at the Inn

Luke 2:7 "And she brought forth her firstborn son, and wrapped him in swaddling clothes, and laid him in a manger; because there was no room for them in the inn."

No room at the inn for the expectant mother; no room at the inn for the weary father. No comfort for them.

Chosen of God to bring His son into a world that was undone. No room at the inn for the travailing mother; no one cared if she were to suffer.

Off to the stable they plodded along, preparing to birth God's only son. God's only son, born in a stable, came to give life to those who are able.

No room at the inn; no comfort for them. Yet, He came to die for all men.

Additional Scriptures: Luke 2:7-14, Matthew 1:20-25

Rejoice

2 Peter 1:19 (NIV) "And we have the word of the prophets made more certain, and you will do well to pay attention to it, as a light shining in a dark place, until the day dawns and the morning star rises in your hearts."

Someday my night of trials shall fade into the morning star's light; and day's dawn will rise in my heart. On that day, I will absorb His glory into the very depths of my being.

Then shall I toss my cup of sorrows to the sun's yellow hair and moon's milky beams; and I will dance on clouds of happiness with wings on my feet.

I shall skip over mountains and leap over hills while laughing with the rainbows of my soul. I will gleefully listen for His voice in the rumbling of the thunders and rejoice with Him in the brightness of the lighting.

My soul will then bask in God's healing presence; and I will drink deeply from the purple wine of His Spirit. I shall take immense pleasure in His unending love as I sense His immortality merging into me.

Then I shall be free!

Additional Scriptures: 2 Sam. 22:34-37, 1Peter 1:8-11,
    Psalm 30:5

Our Relationship with Jesus

Matthew 5:6-8 (KJV) "Blessed are they which do hunger and thirst after righteousness: for they shall be filled. Blessed are the merciful: for they shall obtain mercy. Blessed are the pure in heart: for they shall see God."

Christianity differs with other religions because Christianity is more than a religion. It is a relationship. Those who will, enter into an intimate friendship with the Lord and giver of all life. As with any relationship, a relationship with Christ requires communication. It is essential to the Christian life to speak to our Father and to listen for His still small voice. The Scripture instructs us to persist in our prayers, to ask that His will be done on earth as it is in heaven, and to pray for both provision and forgiveness. The Scripture also instructs us to study to show ourselves approved.

We begin our relationship with the Lord by inviting Him into our hearts and lives. We worship, pray, and read His word to grow in closeness to Him. Our servanthood also involves entering into relationship with those who are of the household of faith. It is through these interactions that we exhort, encourage, and inspire one another.

Our fellowship with the Lord begins as we enter into a relationship with Him and our new life begins as we walk into that place of perfection in Christ. I think it's time to have that talk with Jesus.

Additional Scriptures: Psalms 119:2-7 & 73-77, Psalms 55:1,
    2Timothy 2:15

Calvary

John 19:15-19 "But they cried out, Away with him, away with him, crucify him. Pilate saith unto them, Shall I crucify your King? The chief priests answered, we have no king but Caesar. Then delivered he him therefore unto them to be crucified. And they took Jesus, and led him away. And he bearing his cross went forth into a place called the place of a skull, which is called in the Hebrew Golgotha: Where they crucified him, and two other with him, on either side one, and Jesus in the midst. And Pilate wrote a title, and put it on the cross. And the writing was JESUS OF NAZARETH THE KING OF THE JEWS."

Had I been there on Calvary, had I the revelation of Jesus Christ in me, I would have knelt upon the ground and worshipped the man in the thorny crown.

Had I been there at Calvary, had I the love of God in me, I would have plead unto the crowd; "Remove this man; He has no sin."

Had I been there on Calvary, had I seen Christ hanging from that rugged tree, I would have cried, "Please take Him down; remove the man with the thorny crown."

Had I been there on Calvary and watched as Jesus died for me, I would have wept and praised the Lord, for sin in me would dwell no more.

Additional Scriptures: Psalm 22:16-18, Psalms 69:21

Color Him Crimson

John 19:2 (NIV) "The soldiers twisted together a crown of thorns and put it on his head. They clothed him in a purple robe."

Color Him crimson for the blood He shed
Color Him purple, place a crown on His head
Color Him sad, rejected, and alone
Color Him forgiving for sins atoned
Color Him compassionate and healer too
Color Him, color Him in every hue

Color Him Savior, redeemer of the lost
Color Him selfless, He died on the cross
Color Him restorer for all that's wrong
Color Him friend and eternal too
Color Him, color Him in every hue

Additional Scriptures: John 19:2-5, Esther 8:15, Isaiah 28:5

When Life Throws You a Curve Ball

1 John 2:1-2 "My little children, these things write I unto you, that ye sin not. And if any man sin, we have an advocate with the Father, Jesus Christ the righteous: And he is the propitiation for our sins: and not for ours only, but also for the sins of the whole world."

When I was about seven years old, my parents coaxed my older sister Alana to teach me how to play baseball. This was no small feat for me, coordination not being one of my gifts. However, Alana was a superior athlete and was more than willing to show her little sister just how it was done. At one point during my lesson, I decided to stand directly behind Alana. I thought I could more easily decipher just how she was swinging that bat and connecting with the baseball. I'll tell you what: she swung that bat with all her might and every ounce of her athletic talent thrown in for good measure. I took the full impact of that swing in my stomach. Immediately, I fell backwards onto my father's immaculately groomed clover and gasped desperately for breath. I wasn't in pain; I was just desperate for a breath of air.

I had forgotten all about this experience until the other day. My husband came home from work and related some difficult news concerning a family member. I began gasping for breath, desperate for some air. I could hear my husband in the background saying, "Breathe, Pam, breathe." I didn't know what to do with myself. Had I caused this, had he; what should we do? Suddenly, I realized that I have an advocate with the Father. There was no need to try and fix the blame or even the problem. I needed only to ask Him and He would give me peace and carry me through the storm. And peace was given, for I have an advocate with the Father.

Additional Scriptures: Romans 5:1-5, Matthew 8:26-27

Steadfast Love

2 Corinthians 8:9 (KJV) "For you know the grace of our Lord Jesus Christ, that though he was rich, yet for your sakes he became poor, so that you through his poverty might become rich."

Psalm 108:1(KJV) "O God, my heart is steadfast; I will sing and give praise, even with my glory."

> I must stand still and listen
> For I am lost on how to handle
> This matter.
>
> Wait, I hear the answer.
> The only way out
> Is to follow
> The blood-stained footsteps,
> There is no other.
>
> Stopping, I look behind
> I see the ease
> Because He Loves with a
> Steadfast
> Love.

Confused?
There is no other way
Just follow His footsteps
To the cross.

Additional Scriptures: Psalm 57:7, Psalm 112:7,
John 1:40-42

The Keeper

Psalm 121:1-3 (KJV) "I will lift up mine eyes unto the hills from whence cometh my help. My help cometh from the LORD, which made heaven and earth. He will not suffer thy foot to be moved: he that keepeth thee will not slumber."

I have always enjoyed the stunning mountains that surround Tucson, Arizona. When our four children were little, on days when the mountains were especially beautiful, I would holler, "Hurry kids, come and look at my mountains." My kids never disappointed me. They always ran to see the purple mountain majesties with the sun shinning on them in a certain way, or to see the fresh snow on top of Mt. Lemon.

I didn't realize how much I had personalized those mountains until one day our youngest son ran in from playing outdoors and said, "Quick mommy, come look at your mountains!" My mountains indeed. Although I don't personally possess those mountains, I certainly own the view.

Many times I would look to those mountains and remember the words of David the psalmist, "I will lift up mine eyes unto the hills from whence cometh my help. My help cometh from the Lord." Resting my eyes on those mountains made me aware that there was someone much greater than me taking care of my family. I could find rest in His promises knowing that He that keepeth us never sleeps or fails us.

Additional Scriptures: Psalms 121:1-8, Matthew 14:23

Wings of Morning

Psalms 18:10 (KJV) "And he rode upon a cherub, and did fly:
yea, he did fly upon the wings of the wind."

> Should you fly upon the wings of the wind and ride high
> above life's tempestuous seas, His eye would be upon thee.
> Were you then to dash into a chariot of fire led by
>   prancing
> stallions and race the wind to the earth's very end, He
>   would
> go before thee.
>
> Should you then be given the opportune to skip upon
>   the dust
> of the moon, He would be there in all power and glory
> controlling the earth's ebb and flow with perfect authority.
>
> Were you then to take up a harp and play majestically,
> He would be there cheering you on and giving you love for
> lost humanity.
>
> And in the end, when you shall be waltzing through
>   rainbows
> of joy and floating on galaxies of peace, He shall be there

too, holding out His silver chalice of all things wise and wonderful for you.

Additional Scriptures: Jude 1:25, Daniel 3:15 (a),
   Daniel 7:14

On Prayer

Daniel 9:23 (MSG) "You had no sooner started your prayer when the answer was given. And now I'm here to deliver the answer to you. You are much loved!"

A little prayer for those who read this "baby" devotional book. And for my dear friend Pat, who cried when she got this poem on her birthday:

> If my prayers could be a butterfly today,
> I would spread my wings and fly your way.
>
> I would hover about and sweeten your life.
> I would take away your tears and calm
> your mind.
>
> If my prayers could a butterfly be, I would
> take your hurts and fulfill all your dreams.
>
> I would sprinkle some joy over your life and
> flutter about for your delight.
>
> If my prayers were a butterfly today, I would
> Spread my wings and come your way.

Of course, as much as I wish I could do these things for you, I can't, but I know Someone who can. Won't you turn your problems over to Him today?

Additional Scriptures: Daniel 9:17-18, and
    Colossians 1:9-12

"What the catepillar thinks is the end......the butterfly knows is only the beginning." Anon.

Firelight

1Peter 1:7 "That the trial of your faith, being much more precious than of gold that perisheth, though it be tried with fire, might be found unto praise and honour and glory at the appearing of Jesus Christ:"

"Only the fire born can understand blue." Carl Sandburg

> FIRELIGHT,
> Color it orange, yellow, blue and bright.
> FIRELIGHT,
> Illuminates, imprints, and scars.
> FIRELIGHT,
> Creates agony beyond belief.
> FIRELIGHT brings,
> Understanding, compassion, and empathy
> For others who have also passed through the fire.
> EXPERIENCES….beyond deception.

Thank you, Lord, for bringing us through our trials and for the times that You have put us in a place where looking up and trusting You was our only way out.

Additional Scriptures: Daniel 3:26-28

On Compassion and Tolerance

1 John 3:17 (KJV) " But whoso hath this world's good, and seeth his brother have need, and shutteth up his bowels of compassion from him, how dwelleth the love of God in him?"

"How far you go in life depends on being tender with the young, compassionate with the aged, sympathetic with the striving, and tolerant of the weak and the strong. Because someday in life you will have been all of these." George Washington Carver

Wow, what an insightful paragraph Mr. Carver wrote. He says so much in a concise, profound manner. I think Mr. Carver had a certain knack for getting to the point.

Lord, I know that you have the power to give me the grace to be tender, compassionate, sympathetic, and tolerant. It's a tall order, but You're *The Man,* the Giver of attributes, the Author of life. I pray that You will do this work in me. Thank you, Lord, for answering my prayers today and sending me on the journey of life.

Additional Scriptures: Luke 19:41, Proverbs 19:17,
    Isaiah 9:36, 40:11, 50:4-5, 53:4a,

The Un-birthday

Jeremiah 29:11 (ESV) "For I know the plans I have for you, declares the LORD, plans for wholeness and not for evil, to give you a future and a hope."

This year I decided that my birthday would just quietly pass by, an un-birthday if you will. I informed my friends and family that this was a birthday to ignore. After all, I've had a lot of birthdays, and this particular one didn't end in a 0, or even a 5, so why bother?

God, it would seem, had different plans. I had an incredible birthday, one that will always stand out in my mind. It started early on my birthday when I got a call to be a substitute teacher at a local high school in the Special Ed. Department.

This class had several Down's syndrome students, who began their day by getting up in front of the class one at a time, and talking about what was going on in their lives. The students held a rather large stuffed, green frog for confidence while they spoke. I learned about their suppers, favorite TV programs, their siblings, and parents.

I never dreamed they would call on me to speak. There wasn't any performance anxiety coming from my corner. However, I must have looked a little too happy, because one of the students tossed me the huge, green frog, signaling it was my turn to speak. Up I went to talk about my day. The students were extremely responsive to everything I said. Before I sat down, the class insisted on singing happy birthday to me (woops, it was supposed to be a un-birthday…I must have slipped). What a pleasure it was to see those bright, shinning faces singing to me so sincerely and lovingly. A birthday blessing I won't soon forget. Those children gave me some of the greatest gifts anyone could ever give: love, acceptance, and precious memories.

Additional Scriptures: Ephesians 1:3, Proverb 27:9

On Friendship

Proverbs 17:17 (KJV) "A friend loves at all times, and a brother is born for adversity." Proverbs 27:9 (NKJV) "Ointment and perfume delight the heart, And the sweetness of a man's friend *gives delight* by hearty counsel."

"Friendship is a sheltering tree." Samuel Coleridge

Father, you bestow many gifts upon us. Your Son is the greatest gift, beyond anything these human words can express. And then you give us family to delight, encourage, strengthen and, yes, sometimes even challenge us. Friends are the icing on the cake. They are there to celebrate life's milestones with us, affirm and encourage us when we are down, and be our family when none is around.

Today, my wonderful friend Heather called. She lives out of state, and our conversations are few and far between. Heather, as usual, was filled with Your love, compassion, and that wonderful, upbeat, full-of- joy Heather way.

I hope, dear readers, that you are thinking of Heather in your life. If not, ask the Giver of all good gifts to place someone in your life who will affirm and love you where you are at. One person can make a difference, for "friendship is a sheltering tree."

Additional Scriptures: Proverb 18:24, Proverb 13:20, Proverb 27:9

Peace

Revelation 1:5 (CEV) "May kindness and **peace** be yours from Jesus Christ, the faithful witness. Jesus was the first to conquer death, and he is the ruler of all earthly kings. Christ loves us, and by his blood he set us free from our sins."

For the shipwrecked who are tossing and turning on life's turbulent sea, turn to the Savior; for He is the Master of peace. He spoke to the wind, "Peace be still," and He can speak to your storm as no other will.

For those who are walking in darkness, ask Him the way; He'll guide your footsteps day by day. He will light a candle of understanding in your heart for the all world to see, the reflection of Christ, which brings peace and harmony.

Additional Scriptures: Phil 4:6-7, Col 3:15,
    Daniel 10:19

The Resurrection

1Corinthians 15:3-4 (KJV) "For I delivered unto you first of all that which I also received, how that Christ died for our sins according to the scriptures; And that he was buried, and that he rose again the third day according to the scriptures:"

I have a most enchanting cousin. Her name is Lily and she is three years old. Lily is extremely precocious and a natural leader.

Lily possesses a glorious head of blonde hair, beautiful eyes and her daddy's heart. She speaks with an adorable raspy voice which she inherited from her Auntie Joyce.

Last Easter she learned about the resurrection during Sunday school. Shortly after Easter her beloved grandfather "Papa" died. Lily repeatedly ask her mother if she could go see Papa. Her mother, Tricha, would say, "Lily, Papa died." Finally Lily, out of exasperation ask her mother, "Well, when is Papa going to be resurrected?"

I wept a little when I heard this story. Isn't it incredible? Out of the mouth of babes.

Additional Scriptures: Ephesians 2:4-6, 1Corin.15:12-19.

About the Author

Pam is a native of Globe, Arizona and resides in Tucson, Arizona. She is the mother of four and grandmother of two. She has enjoyed writing since a college professor turned her on to the joy of writing.

Pam especially likes writing poetry and has received two Editor Choice Awards for her Poetry.

Pam has a Bachelor's degree in Elementary Education and is a substitute teacher. Pam and her husband Mack attend Casas Adobe Baptist Church.

About the Book

This book is a 30 day devotional. It contains inspirational nuggets and poetry. There are scripture references for each day. The devotionals are short and inspirational. This book would make a great gift for someone who is traveling or perhaps a busy housewife who has only snippets of time for reading. It can easily be tucked into a purse or suitcase, to be pulled out and read while waiting at the airport or doctor's office.

Pages for free preview: Color Him Crimson and Calvary

Printed in Great Britain
by Amazon